A Chinese Emperor is
question of the m

He meets an old Sag
surprising methods to
consciousness and catch a glimpse of
the extraordinary ways in which civilizations
rise and fall, one after another, on
this earth...

With the Sage's help, the Emperor begins to
be guided by his intuition, learns to live in
the present and to *Use what he is*...

Fun-Chang

Use What You Are

A Chinese Fable

Translated by Matthew Reisz

EAST-WEST PUBLICATIONS
London and The Hague

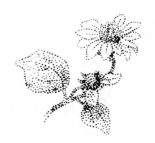

Introduction

This story forms part of the treasury of Ancient Chinese wisdom. It is attributed to Fun-Chang, a writer who lived centuries before the Christian era. Its poetic depth, the simplicity of the lessons it contains, its humour and universally valid message all encouraged us to produce an English adaptation and have it published. As with all folktales, the aim is to affect readers' intuitive and imaginative capabilities. It is a good idea, therefore, to pause occasionally as you read, shut your eyes and project the images it conjures up on to what one might call the interior screen of your closed pupils. Another technique is to let your eyes play with the thousands of little dots which form the illustrations, until they seem to come to life or become like stars in the dreamscape sky.

Some readers will be wondering about the facts: did the Emperor's adventures really take place? Did the city of Loyang exist? Was it destroyed by an earthquake? And what was the old Sage's real name? To answer such questions, we can only repeat the Buddha's words: 'Truth is what is useful.' This remarkable saying reveals that there are no absolute truths, valid for everybody and at all times; rather, ideas are true to the extent that a particular individual finds them useful, at a particular moment of his or her life.

And so, through its teaching of tolerance and respect for different people's individual truths, everyone will discover in this Chinese story both its universal wisdom and what is useful—and hence true—for him or her personally. Yet, like the Emperor in the story, I hope you may learn better how to 'Use what you are' and so create in your daily life a deeper consciousness, happiness and freedom!

The publisher

In Ancient China there lived an Emperor, who kept a close eye on his subjects every day. Through one of the palace windows he could see his grooms looking after the horses, the guards trying out their weapons, and the gardeners hard at work. Through another window he had a good view of the market-place of Loyang, his capital city, and he took a great interest in the way the different people—buyers and sellers, winners and losers—treated each other. Finally, in the evening, he would watch the sweepers clearing up after everybody else had left.

And so he watched, and went on watching day after day... Yet the more he saw and the more he heard, the less he understood!

Two days a week were spent on legal judgements. People from all over China who refused to accept the decisions of their

provincial governors came to Loyang to appeal and were heard in a court of justice where the Emperor presided; his decisions were absolutely binding. Problems of succession, disputes between neighbours, the pleas of people who considered themselves too poor to pay taxes, or of invalids who wanted to be looked after at public expense—all of these issues came before him, as well as conflicts between different towns and provinces. And as he passed judgement, he kept his eyes wide open; for years he carefully observed what was taking place, until suddenly he could bear no longer to wrestle with the questions he kept asking himself, without finding any answers... His ministers could not help him, since they were just like the people who came to demand justice; nor could the sorcerers and magicians, who would want to use magic to *change* reality; even his doctors were people of the same type...

One evening, he was walking in his gardens, recalling all the people he had come across in his life, trying to think of someone who could

help him answer the questions which were making his head spin. He remembered an old Sage he had met in his youth, who knew a great deal...

Was he really a wise man—or had he only *seemed* wise to the youthful Emperor? If only he was there, in the garden, and could respond to all the questions which tore at the Emperor's heart! Hardly had this thought crossed his mind than the old Sage appeared just next to him. The Emperor immediately started firing questions: 'Why are some people born beautiful and others deformed? Why are some people wise and others ignorant? Why does one man become a trader and another an artist? Why don't some people care about improving their lives? Why would the man who sweeps the marketplace refuse a top position at the palace if I offered it to him? Why are some people stronger than others, some rich and some poor? Why is everything as it is? I saw a boy of 15,' the Emperor said, 'the son of one of my ministers, who lost his life when he was playing with friends. Why? Where did his life go—and why was it so short? There are members of my court, on the other hand, who are 90 years old and can hardly move. Why have their lives been so long? I can lay down laws and pass judgements,' said the Emperor, 'but all such questions exceed my understanding.'

The Sage replied: 'Look at your garden!'

The Emperor looked about him and said: 'It is very beautiful!'

'Look at that oak, so majestic in old age, and then consider the gracious young jujube tree. Look at the flowers and plants: some are strong and some weak; some live for decades and others but a year. Some have leaves which have dried out or flowers which have never reached maturity; some of the trees can't develop properly, because the larger trees all round deprive them of sun. Why don't you ask me about flowers, trees and plants?

And then there are animals. Why hasn't a chicken got the strength of a buffalo? Why isn't a tiger as faithful as a dog? Why should an eagle cut through the air with such power while sparrows seem so weak? Isn't it unfair that some living beings are eagles and others sparrows, some blades of grass and others great oaks, that some stones are diamonds and others granite? Don't you find that deeply unjust?' asked the Sage.

'But you're not talking about people!' replied the Emperor, 'about individuals endowed

13

with reason. You've been describing things we step on or eat or which just play a minor role in our lives.'

'Ah well,' said the Sage, 'that's where you're wrong! The life force which flows in a reed is the same as in an oak. It's the same in you and the man who sweeps the marketplace. We call it God, the Divine Breath, the Life Force, Energy, the Universal Power or even the I AM.'

The Emperor scratched his head. 'Now I'm even more confused than before,' he said.

'Come down to the lake with me and sit on that stone,' said the Sage. He stirred up the surface of the water with his hand and it seemed as if thousands of little bells were tinkling all around them. An image appeared in the lake. 'I'm going to take you a long way back in time,' said the Sage, 'before the days of your father, your father's father or even your father's grandfather. I won't give you a complete global picture but a perspective view, a *glimpse* of what man is, and the same for the minerals and planets, the animals and plants.'

Then extraordinary images appeared on the

surface of the lake: objects flying through the air, vehicles carrying men which needed no horses to draw them, huge metal structures gliding through the seas. Men and women were travelling very fast, dressed in costumes utterly different from those the Emperor had known.

'That civilization existed before the one you know today,' explained the Sage. 'Let us look a bit further back in time.' The screen seemed to enlarge and the Emperor saw hundreds of thousands of people scattered across the planet; he saw civilizations which made the people of his own day seem like cavemen... Then he saw a group of men and women who joined forces, held discussions, passed on information about the nature of their own personal energy, and revealed the beauty, warmth, power and awareness which was theirs. Soon they attracted others who were eager to discover in themselves the same self-

understanding, the same freedom to be able
to live *in* the world without being *of* the world.
One night, the little group of men and women

led the people who had joined them to particular places they had chosen in advance. Suddenly, there were flashes of lightning, claps of thunder—and the surface of the earth was utterly transformed: waves several miles high washed over whole countries, earthquakes buried cities miles below the surface, earth or water engulfed great civilizations; huge territories disappeared and new lands came to light.

The Emperor looked on spellbound. He saw that those who had survived were strong and brave; thanks to the people who guided them, they had learned to see and understand *what they really were*. They all possessed a true capacity for living in harmony with themselves and with the objects of their natural surroundings.

Trees, plants and flowers had disappeared, yet seeds were beginning to germinate. It would take them years to reach maturity. In the same way, tiny groups of people were springing up all over the world. Little by little,

children were born. Soon they began to ask questions: 'Where do we come from? Where are we going?' When their parents tried to describe what they had lived through, their children found it difficult to believe. Since no images or objects had survived from the earlier era, how could they explain what it had been like? How could they make their children understand?

Some of the young set off to create new societies elsewhere. Soon the survivors of the earlier era died out. The images on the surface of the lake became confused and then disappeared...

The Sage said to the Emperor: 'Those who survive must go beyond.'

'I don't understand,' said the Emperor.

'The people you saw were wise, because they were guided by their inner resources; they led the survivors to begin a new cycle. Such wise men and women are, in a sense, the food, fuel and energy of each cycle. A supply of energy is needed to bring the cycle of life to completion.

Man is born unable to feed himself and dies in the same condition. Everything that lives lives in cycles; minerals and plants, flowers, animals and men—all live by following the cycles of nature. Even our planet earth pursues its own cycle.

Men and women like them who possess a highly developed sense of themselves and a genuine capacity for unity with every living thing have a role to play whenever a cataclysm shakes the earth. It is they who maintain the necessary cohesion, they who bring the elements which are indispensable for the completion of the global cycle. They don't have to be either good or evil; they are *energy.* They can be popes or emperors, gladiators or shepherds, carters or civil servants; what matters is that they transmit energy. They help the cycle complete itself; they form the bridge between one era and the next, the thread which creates the web of human history.

You must understand, Emperor, that your

street sweeper is like a seed, a potential source of energy; perhaps, in the fullness of time, in another era, he will become a different kind of being, perhaps a tree with powerful branches. For the moment, you must not want him to be other than he is. A large part of wisdom and knowledge consists in just that: accepting people for what they are and understanding *their* experience of life without trying to turn them into what they are not. Do you pull up all the plants in your garden which aren't oaks? No, you try and achieve a harmonious balance between the grass and flowers, trees and bushes. When you water the roses, do you say to them: "I want you to live as long as an oak tree"? Roses don't want to be oak trees; they want to be roses! Why do you require *people* to be other than they are?

This,' the Sage went on, 'is the hardest lesson for humans to learn, but you can start by accepting evolution in the animal, vegetable and mineral kingdoms. You have already come to terms with the fact that a tiger is stronger than a rat, that a cow produces more milk than a chicken. Can't you understand that a street sweeper likes to be a street sweeper? That even those who are hungry form part of your imperial garden? Certainly you can feed them, but that doesn't do justice

to the whole situation. You must learn, Emperor, that it is *not* your job to feed your people; you can make sure that food is available to every citizen, but they have to learn how to feed *themselves*. A civilization which starts feeding its people—on the grounds that they are incapable of providing for themselves—soon runs into trouble. A

person who cannot take care of himself has already started to die. An animal which cannot look after itself becomes another's prey. A plant which isn't strong enough to reach out for the sun and for water returns to the earth whence it came.

Come with me. Go deeper into the image forming before your eyes and look at that forest. It was a magnificent forest, with huge trees, marvellous flowers, animals wandering about in all directions. This part of the forest,' said the Sage, 'has never been touched by the hand of man. Life is everywhere! Look at the grass, flowers and trees, the birds, insects and animals ... They live out their life cycles, they learn and evolve.'

'But,' said the Emperor, 'man is more advanced and intelligent.'

'Who says so?' replied the Sage. 'How do you know if man has a higher or lower place in creation than the minerals? The mineral kingdom never complains, never tries to steal

from others and never kills; its actions possess a sort of simplicity, in accordance with the natural surroundings. Are you *sure* that man occupies a higher place in the universal plan—and that you're not going to evolve into a rock?'

'That seems unthinkable,' replied the Emperor.

'Your thought is limited, and yet anything you imagine can exist. Nothing is impossible.'

'But how does all this help me in my role as Emperor? There have just been more terrible floods in the South; many people have lost their homes and thousands have been drowned; the survivors are crying out for supplies.'

'Have you ever asked yourself, Emperor, why those people live so near the ocean, on river banks or on low-lying land that is easily flooded? Why they build houses on cliffs, which can easily collapse? And why they fight against nature, instead of trying to live in

25

harmony with her? The forces of nature are like a hundred million horsemen armed with sharpened swords; there are no means in the world of resisting them.

Educated men and women know where to live, where to build their houses and how to protect themselves. If they are fishermen, teach them to *use* the winds and tides, how to live *with* nature; if they insist on fighting against her, it is they who must take the consequences. You cannot shed tears at the fate of someone who has lost a house in an earthquake, a flood or a storm. If they choose to live there, it is they who run the risk. You cannot force people to change their lives. When there are too many weeds and not enough oaks, more sparrows than eagles, more rats than tigers, more granite than diamonds, an imbalance is created which brings about an adjustment through the play of natural forces. Nothing dies. Certain forms of life disappear and are replaced by others, but the living spirit in all of them never dies. Funerals are held for the living, not the dead. Survivors may welcome the chance to express their grief, but corpses don't care—especially since they aren't really dead but continuing their life in some other form. Forests and flowers don't hold funerals, and nor do animals, birds and insects.'

'I have been a bad emperor!' said the Emperor.

'No!' said the Sage, 'You have *not* been a bad emperor! You have used the means you possessed. Within the limits of your understanding, you used your abilities as best you could and you've been capable of learning. Through your every action, the energy within you has revealed itself.'

The old Sage would have liked the Emperor to see and understand more, but he knew that understanding can only dawn slowly. The Emperor asked: 'What about the laws of the country? Should I scrap them all and start from scratch?'

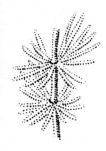

'No,' said the Sage, 'control the people in your empire as a gardener controls his garden. A gardener allows his plants to grow without trying to force them to become what they're not. When I see the rock you're sitting on, I wouldn't go up to it and say: "I don't like the way you are! I don't like your colour! You'd better become a jade rock!" The gardener doesn't tell the bird in the tree: "You ought to be an eagle! I'm going to turn you into an eagle!" You *can't* turn a sparrow into an eagle nor a street sweeper into an emperor, just as you can't make everyone happy. Each individual is like a vibration, an energy which chooses a body, lives within it and uses it as a means. In your dining room you use cutlery; your stable boy just uses his hands. If he came to eat with you, you'd both fill your bellies in the same way, yet he'd need a bath afterwards and you'd still be clean! It's the same with energy: it enters a body which looks much like any other. Observe the ministers you have about you at court: with

29

very rare exceptions, they all have two arms,
two legs and two eyes. They all have more
or less the same body, and yet they're all

different. Why is one a deep thinker and not another? How does your magician move objects around the room by force of will? Each person is an energy, and the energy in each causes *everything* which happens within him. It does so by making use of the experiences a person has lived through at every stage of his life.'

'Do you mean to say that I have already lived on earth in a previous existence?'

'In a certain sense, yes,' said the Sage. 'That's one way of looking at the question, yet the most important thing to understand is that next time round your energy will be capable of absorbing something new.'

'But how can something evil be a useful energy?' asked the Emperor.

'What you call "evil" is an energy. You can kill thousands of people, even millions, without that being "evil".'

'How can that be?'

'Why should that be bad? Why should it be evil? You crush thousands of flies, kill thousands of animals and plants for food. What is the difference between their energy and a man's?'

'But a man is one of my own kind!'

'Don't you think a tomato could say the same thing about another tomato? It is important

to understand that. There is no need to preach or to try and teach others such wisdom. What you must do is observe things, so that they become part of your being. Then you'll be able to live in the world without fear, frustration or anger, and without passing judgement—because you'll have learnt to observe. There is immense power in being

able to witness everything that happens without becoming involved in it. Look at the oak which dominates the garden and the birds which nest in its branches. Or look at the eagle which observes everything that takes place on the ground below. Remember that people must draw lessons from what they live through. If you have regrets or pity others, you identify yourself with them and become a part of what *they* are—you won't be allowing *your own* energy to develop to the full.'

'But what *is* energy?' asked the Emperor.

'Ah, I'll talk to you about that later. First, you need the basic knowledge and to understand what you are.'

'You have shown me great upheavals taking place on earth. Will I live to see such events? And what will they be like?'

'Exactly the same as before.'

'Will there be a group of sages who know in advance what will happen?'

'Yes.'

'Will they prepare other people for what will happen?'

'Yes.'

'Will I be part of that group?'

'Maybe—and maybe not!'

'Then I could perish if I don't attain a certain degree of wisdom?'

'You won't perish but you'll be renewed. For example, if you were an oak at the time and your lower trunk was in a poor state, you would feel the need to be renewed. And the same applies if you are an old eagle who can no longer fly or a diamond so full of cracks it has lost all its strength. The diamond was once really a diamond, the eagle an eagle and the oak an oak, yet each is ready for new experiences. You must learn to use your power; to use it to the full, you must not let others' energy control your own. You can try and understand other people and even learn

from them, but remember always to remain an observer.'

'But what am I to think about all you've taught me? How do I know you're not trying to lead me astray, deceive me or make fun of me?'

'And what would I do that for? I've got nothing to gain,' said the Sage. 'I don't want to become emperor; you're not going to give me great riches. I wouldn't give a fig for that! Don't talk to anyone about what you've just learnt. Keep it to yourself. It is your interior visions, intuitions and inspirations which are your jewels and diamonds. Let them become your strength and achievement.

When you are seated at court and many people come before you, observe them carefully. If they come from an area which has been flooded, educate them; if they come to ask for money, teach them to work. Don't try to do *for them* what they must do for themselves. Then I'll be able to show you the light, energy and resources of your being which you haven't discovered up until now.'

'But I want to know about them!'

'I could list them for you in various ways,' said the Sage, 'but can a troop of elephants fit into a small room? You must understand that I have told you everything you will be able to absorb for the moment. Teaching has to proceed step by step: as you grow up and allow your body, heart and brain to work better, I will be able to bring you more; the more you receive, the better you will understand those around you and the natural world which surrounds us all. Would you stay under a tree which is about to fall down?'

'Of course not,' said the Emperor, 'What a ridiculous question!'

'And what if you didn't know the tree was about to fall?'

'Oh,' said the Emperor, 'you mean that I *should* know if the tree is going to fall?'

'You can become part of everything,' said the Sage. 'When an infirm old woman comes before you, don't put her into an old people's home. Help her to learn to use what she is. If her legs can hardly move and she can't bend her arms and you say to her: "Old woman, you have had a long life, you need someone to look after you. I'm going to lodge you in a sunny rest home in the South," she'll be happy—but a hundred other old women will come and ask for help! If, on the other hand, you say: "Tomorrow you're going to have a cold bath, learn to run and get your body working!" then she'll get better, but you won't have a crowd of old women rushing up to become dependent on you! You must help people to help themselves. You provide the means, knowing full well that they have the capacity to use them.'

'Teach me to use *your* means!' said the Emperor.

'How can I teach you to use instruments

which need seven hands to pick up?'

'But what do *you* do then?' asked the Emperor.

'That's easy,' said the Sage—and suddenly he had seven hands!

'Oh,' said the Emperor, 'I couldn't do that.'

'And yet you could,' said the Sage. 'Anything you can conceive of, you can achieve.'

The Emperor looked at the lake and began to reflect. Everything he had heard was so new—and yet so important! He was sure that his new understanding was going to transform his life and that he would help other people to transform their own, even though he could not do it for them. He turned towards the old Sage and said: 'When I look at the marketplace, I've noticed that much of the buying and selling takes place in one particular area. When people leave for the evening, some of them fall over and get hurt. I ought to post a guard there to maintain order.'

'You want to protect them?' asked the Sage. '*Why* do you want to protect them?'

'So they can return home unhurt.'

'You must think they are complete idiots, unable to do anything for themselves! How many laws have you made on the grounds that your subjects aren't able to look after themselves?'

'But if there weren't any laws there would be complete chaos!' said the Emperor.

'You're right: the more people there are, the more laws are needed. And yet *you* must learn how to live and function without laws. You must learn to live in a world governed by one supreme Law. Wherever you look in nature, the same Law applies.'

'Teach it to me,' said the Emperor.

'I can teach you how to live above and beyond laws,' said the Sage, 'although you must continue to pass laws for the people around you who cannot yet do without them. Can you live with that idea?'

The Emperor thought for a moment and then said: 'I don't know.'

'It's very simple,' the Sage told him, 'the eagle in the sky cannot swim in the sea; fish don't fly through the air; and butterflies don't take pollen from the jujube tree. All of them use their own energy. You must lay down laws for others, although you yourself are beyond them. Because people have no intuitive understanding and are unable to live naturally, they need you to make laws for them. Plants and animals, reeds and rocks, all know how to live. They can feel when an earthquake is coming or when a storm is on the way and they act accordingly. A plant which lives by the sea makes sure that its roots go deep, so the wind can't tear it out. A man who can listen to his intuition has no need of laws.'

'But not everybody can have intuition,' said the Emperor.

'We'll talk about that tomorrow!' said the Sage. 'Wait a moment,' said the Emperor. 'You have spoken to me about the men and women wise and strong who are like the threads which create the web of life. You have told me that if I express the energy within me, my body may become stronger and my understanding more profound. But how will I know when I have experienced everything and no longer need to continue my bodily existence?'

'When the time comes, believe me, you will know!' said the Sage. 'Yet as long as you ask me questions like that, the time has not yet come.'

The Emperor returned to his bedroom. He had spent the whole day in the garden with the old Sage and it felt as if he'd been there for weeks. He had seen, heard and absorbed as much as he could. He lay down on his bed, pulled up the blankets and fell asleep. Immediately he was overcome by dreams: he was himself walking in a forest, among the trees, birds and insects; he felt the forest shaking, as if a giant was walking nearby; animals ran off in every direction, birds were thrown into the air, the forest continued to shake—and he was afraid. Then, as the forest was becoming ever more agitated, the Emperor suddenly woke up. His palace was shaking. The doors had fallen down, cracks were appearing in the collapsing walls. He heard shouts coming from the city of Loyang. He wanted to stand up, but the seismic waves kept him glued to the floor and he could only move about on all fours.

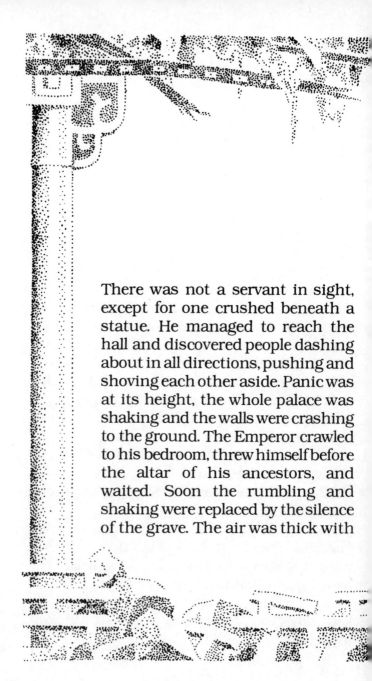

There was not a servant in sight, except for one crushed beneath a statue. He managed to reach the hall and discovered people dashing about in all directions, pushing and shoving each other aside. Panic was at its height, the whole palace was shaking and the walls were crashing to the ground. The Emperor crawled to his bedroom, threw himself before the altar of his ancestors, and waited. Soon the rumbling and shaking were replaced by the silence of the grave. The air was thick with

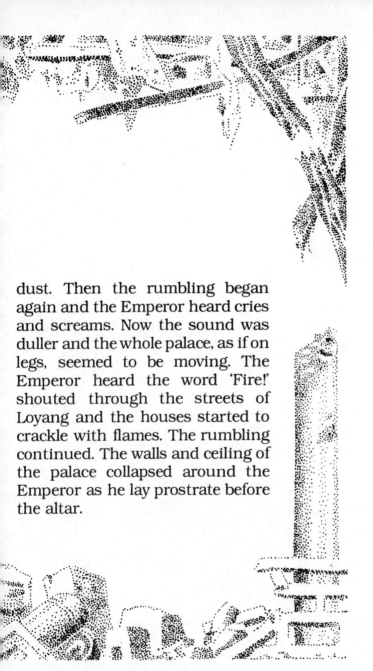

dust. Then the rumbling began again and the Emperor heard cries and screams. Now the sound was duller and the whole palace, as if on legs, seemed to be moving. The Emperor heard the word 'Fire!' shouted through the streets of Loyang and the houses started to crackle with flames. The rumbling continued. The walls and ceiling of the palace collapsed around the Emperor as he lay prostrate before the altar.

He neither prayed nor spoke; yet had he been ready for the next life, he felt, now would have been the perfect time to go! There was a delay which seemed like an eternity and then the rumbling stopped. He waited. Nothing else fell. He carefully stood up and saw around him the granite and marble debris, broken statues, collapsed walls and columns.

He heard a woman calling for help from the Empress's bedroom. He was unable to pull her out from the wreckage and, since there was not a soul in sight to help him, he had to leave her. He went out on to the balcony, now missing its balustrade, and looked out over the city of Loyang: only ruins remained; buildings razed to the ground were being consumed by fires. Tears poured from his eyes and he wondered how many of his other cities had also been destroyed. Was this the

end of the world, the great cataclysm the Sage
had talked about the day before? What could
have caused such an immense disaster, such
ferocity in nature? Why had so many limbs
been crushed beneath huge stones, why were
so many people running in panic through the
streets with their clothes on fire? He felt
desperate and powerless. What could he do?
Where could he begin?

As he walked through the palace, he realized
that it no longer mattered that he was
Emperor of China. Everyone thought only of
their own suffering, misery and fear. He
climbed over the main gate of the palace,
walked through Loyang, and met people who
seemed to be stumbling through fog. No-one
recognized him. He tried to help someone,
but the man started screaming so loud the
Emperor had to back away and leave him.

What could he do? He tried to carry a child to safety, but the child cried and hit out and the Emperor was forced to take him back to the ruined building where its father and mother lay buried. A few soldiers were looting. The Emperor ordered them to stop, but his clothes were covered in dust and they did not recognize him. When they drew their swords, he had to run for his life.

In an instant the earth had buried his capital, deprived him of all power and made everyone crazed with fear and despair. The Emperor returned to his palace, stepping over bodies and rocks and passing ruined buildings which were still on fire. He climbed over collapsed walls and went into his garden. By a miracle, it was completely unharmed: not a flower or drop of water was missing, as if the giant hand which devastated everything all round had spared a single spot. He drank water from the stream, sat on the ground and wept warm tears. How useless he felt, without an army or minister, his Empress wife crushed to death in the palace, his children missing and Loyang devastated! What did he rule over now? And what had happened to the rest of China? He no longer had any power. The army, completely out of control, spent its time pillaging and pilfering. How could he find out if the southern provinces had remained faithful to him, how could he let his subjects know he was still alive? He burst into tears and cried—more bitterly than ever before.

Suddenly he shuddered; he felt a hand on his shoulder and the old Sage stood by his side. The Emperor felt desperately angry and started to shout: 'Look, the palace and town are destroyed, my wife and children dead! An earthquake has devastated the power of my

nation. Your precious nature has destroyed everything! There is nothing left and I am utterly worthless!'

The Sage looked him in the eyes.

The Emperor shouted and shook his fists; he almost wanted to hit the Sage, but a mysterious force prevented him raising his arm. There was another earthquake and he passed out.

The Sage sat beside him, waited for him to regain consciousness and then asked: 'What are you going to do?'

The Emperor, in despair, shrugged his shoulders and said: 'I don't know.'

'What do you mean by "I don't know"? Your body's alive, you have work to do and a role to play!'

The Emperor cried out: 'I've got nothing left! All my money is buried deep beneath the palace; I can't pay the soldiers, who are looting the city. I have no idea the state the rest of China is in. What can I do?'

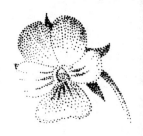

The Sage stood up and said: 'Get up!'
The Emperor got up.
'Look at that eagle in the sky.'
The Emperor raised his eyes. 'Which eagle?'
The Sage pushed him into the river. The water was cold and the Emperor got a shock. He looked at the old Sage and began to laugh: 'Only you would treat me like that! Only you let me feel that I'm a human being. Help me.'
'What do you want to know?' asked the Sage.
'Help me—to rebuild the palace and the city.'
'I cannot help you,' replied the Sage.
'What do you mean by that?'
'I am a Sage. I can see the past and the future. I can understand what is taking place, but I cannot help you.'
The Emperor said: 'I don't understand.'
The Sage continued: 'A seer can only see. He can help others use the means they possess, but he can't force them; he certainly cannot do the work in their stead.'
'Why am I here?' asked the Emperor. 'Why

was I put on this earth—what's the use of it all? We come here, die, return, die again—it's absolutely crazy! Look at all that devastation!' The Sage said: 'Don't seek to know why you are here; that has absolutely no importance.' The Emperor cried out: 'I need to know why I'm here or I can't rebuild anything and start anew.'

'That's absurd,' said the Sage. 'Does a small child ask why he's here before he learns to walk? Does a newborn baby ask why he was born before he starts to drink? Does he ask where he came from before he learns to speak? Don't be so stupid! You don't need to know where you come from. Lots of people use these mental games to avoid looking themselves in the face, to avoid using the means they have at their disposal. They run away from the reality in front of their noses by saying to themselves "If only I knew where I come from, I would be able to do something." It makes no sense! Ideas like that are no more use than Loyang is today; they're just a form of escape.'

The Emperor was annoyed. 'Do *you* know where I come from and why I am here?' he asked.

'Yes,' said the Sage, 'but if I gave you an intellectual understanding of your situation, it wouldn't help you at all to rebuild Loyang.'

The Emperor replied: 'Then what *do* I need to know?'

'You need to know that you have to live out the particular situation in which you find yourself. You can stay here indefinitely gazing at your navel and repeating to yourself: "Why has this happened to me? Why have I come here? Where have I come from? Why has this happened to me? Why has my family been destroyed? Why am I Emperor of China?" All these questions are meaningless. You are here—*that's* all that matters. You *are* Emperor of China. What are you going to *do* with that fact? You can stay

here snivelling and whining, but that won't take you a step forward. You are here because you are here and you must use the situation as best you can. Stop making excuses for yourself!'

The Emperor was mortified. The old Sage could feel his fear, anger and frustration and said: 'Most people are like little children: *they* don't ask where they come from and where they are going; they only think of walking, eating and experiencing life. Some people reach the threshold of thought and start to ask themselves questions. Some find religion or a master who gives them answers, but there are also some like you who wish to know more, to understand all the details. I could give you a thousand explanations and dazzle you so much you would be disgusted by your own feeble attempts at reasoning. But what good would that do you? What could you make of it? Do you give your son a ton of rice to eat at one go?'

'No,' said the Emperor.

'But he'll easily eat that much during his lifetime. Why don't you give it to him all at once so he no longer needs to eat?'

'But that would kill him!'

'Ah,' said the Sage, 'you have understood. You mustn't ask yourself a lot of useless questions but use the situation you are in. Don't say to yourself: "If only I had turned left instead of right, it wouldn't have happened; if only I had sent my children to the summer palace, they might still be alive." Such soul-searching leads nowhere. You are where you are now and it's there you must be. You can't live either in the past or future but in the present. Whatever your situation, use the means you have at your disposal—your hands, intelligence and strength.'

'But I don't *have* the means, I can't even build a house.'

The old Sage shook his head. 'Fear and terror have added to your ignorance. Your means are anything you use to get some work done, even a word or a smile. They include your ability to understand that the place where you are now is the place you must be—not in another place or another situation. Use each moment.'

'What would have happened if I'd been killed?' asked the Emperor.

'What a stupid question!' said the Sage. 'In that case I wouldn't be talking to you and you wouldn't have any problems! Someone else would have come to look after China and you'd be sleeping with your ancestors.'

The Emperor walked around the garden with his hands behind his back looking thoughtfully at the ground. He turned to the Sage and said: 'Never mind why I'm here, I've got work to do.'

'That's good,' said the Sage.

'Never mind where I'm going, I must put one foot in front of the other.'

'That's good!'

The Emperor slowly advanced a little further.

'But how can I do anything? What means can I use?'

The Sage replied: 'You have covered a distance of nine metres in the last few minutes; in the course of those nine metres you have come across many means!'

The Emperor looked at him. 'Really?' He turned round and looked at the little path which snaked through the garden. 'What means are there?' He turned to right and left and tried to find them. 'Show me!'

'There are fruit on the trees to feed you,' said the Sage.

'Ah yes!' said the Emperor.

'Water to quench your thirst.'

'Oh yes!' said the Emperor. He looked around and then said: 'Wood and stones to build with.'

'That's good,' said the Sage.

The Emperor noticed the birds, the insects, the life buzzing all around him. He wandered here and there in a state of great excitement, observing the everyday things he had found a way of using.

'You're beginning to understand,' said the Sage. 'Use what is there. Most people never see that. They go through life looking for something else, convinced that their objective is very distant when the things they need to achieve their aim are all around them.'

'One moment,' said the Emperor. 'I don't understand.'

'It's simple,' said the Sage. 'If you want to build a wall, what do you need?'

'Stones,' said the Emperor.

'That's right. So where are they?'

'Right here, all around me.'

'That's right—start building!'

'But I need a means of moving the stones!'

'You've just passed something suitable next to the path,' said the Sage.

The Emperor retraced his steps and found a stick which could help lift the stones. 'As well as rocks, I need sand, water and clay to make cement.'

'That's right,' said the Sage, 'and all of them are available to you. Near the little stream you'll find sand and clay.'

The Emperor went and brought back what he needed. 'Now,' said the Sage, 'you have all the means you need to make a wall.'

The Emperor cried out: 'You mean that if we look around and make full use of what is there, all we need to do is get together the

necessary ingredients? And that there's no need to go a long way because everything we require is already close at hand?'

'Yes,' said the Sage, 'every man and woman is able to see, perceive and become united with everything that lives, provided they are conscious of what is around them, rocks, flowers and grass. You can't learn such things if you lock yourself away in a monastery or a laboratory, pursue a single path or use only one method to observe reality. *Your* task is to help others see for themselves, to provide the inspiration for them to start the work of reconstruction.'

The Emperor felt full of enthusiasm. 'Use the means all around you,' said the Sage. 'Use the energy of those who work with you. How many people have you misused in the past? How many have you allowed to deteriorate through non-use?'

The Emperor thought: 'I had a messenger who was very fit when I became Emperor and

could dash from one side of town to another to deliver a message. Then he became a friend; when I needed him recently to deliver a message for me, he was far less agile and could no longer run as fast. And all because I had stopped using him!'

The Emperor went up to a hole in the wall and looked at the devastated city of Loyang. Tears poured from his eyes. 'Wait a minute!' said the Sage. 'Why are you crying?'

'Because of all the people and beauty which were once there.'

'Forget all that!' said the Sage. 'People were nourished by and lived on that beauty, so it was well used. Now use what there *is* and stop looking behind you. Nothing has ever been or will ever be better than the present moment. Every instant in the future will always be "now", since one can only live in the present.'

'Oh,' said the Emperor, and he felt as if he had suddenly acquired forty years of understanding. 'Where should I begin?' he thought. He neither felt, nor saw, nor knew where to start. He turned towards the Sage and said: 'My family has been destroyed.'

'That's good,' said the Sage.

'That's *good*?' demanded the Emperor. '*Why* is that good?'

'Because they were part of one era of your life and you are now living in another. What do you think of your grandfather?' asked the Sage.

'He was an admirable man,' said the Emperor.

'Do you mourn for the fact he is no longer with us?'

'No,' said the Emperor.

'Why?'

And thus the Emperor began to understand.

'Fear, grief and emotion,' said the Sage, 'form a stage in man's evolution, but it is a stage you must go beyond. As long as you are prey to such feelings, you cannot use what you are. Wise men—men who can help people see what they are—don't let themselves get caught up by what has been. They concentrate on the present moment. They can see the past and future but are not led astray by

either.' Hardly had he finished saying these words than the Sage suddenly disappeared.

*
* *

The Emperor began to pace round and round in circles. He was afraid. What was he to do?

He left the garden, went through the palace and reached Loyang. He started to pull the corpses out from under collapsed buildings, piled them up and tried to identify them; soon an old man came to help him. Then a crippled child also joined them and slowly a small group was formed. They set off through the streets of Loyang, piled up the corpses, tried to identify them and then burnt them. An old woman joined the team, and then a soldier who was completely distraught at the loss of his family and needed to keep busy. They found a loving mother who could look after the severely injured and they all went on working tirelessly day after day. Soon other groups were formed and little by little they managed to clean up the town...

Days became weeks and they did not weary. Two or three hundred people showed their strength and courage as they began to re-establish a vibration in the place. One day a soldier recognized the Emperor and

announced his presence to the others. It was a sign of hope: people believed anything was possible since the Emperor was there with them, living with them and eating the same food.

Two weeks later, they heard a noise coming from the hill above the town and they saw a huge army approaching. The Emperor slowly set out to meet them; his face was dirty, his clothes torn, and behind him came the little band of survivors from Loyang. The commander in chief got down from his horse and spoke to the Emperor: 'What has happened here? We've had no news of Loyang for a long time and we thought that invaders must have captured it. We felt the earth quake, but we weren't sure exactly where it happened.'

The general looked at the ruined palace and town and spoke to the old man who stood before him: 'Are you in charge here?'

The Emperor smiled and replied: 'No, we all work together!'

Behind him, someone leapt to his feet and said to the general: 'That man is your Emperor!'

The general looked closely at the old man and noticed a scar he himself had made when he was playing as a child with the young Emperor. He fell to his knees, but the Emperor said: 'Stand up again, take off your armour, and bring your army to help us rebuild Loyang.' They entered the town and the Emperor taught them to use every means available. He dealt with every situation by employing the materials they had at their disposal. If a problem arose and someone said: 'We can't do that!' the Emperor never panicked but simply said 'Let's see.' And on the way an idea would occur to him, a thought would form in his mind, so that when he reached the scene, he had already found a solution within himself.

Months went by. Loyang returned to life and the Emperor took up residence in a little house in his garden. He had used all the granite and marble from his former palace in rebuilding the city. A trader, for example, had used marble from the imperial bedroom to build his house, a dyer was working in a room made from the stones of the great hall, and an invalid used the royal throne as his seat. As he stood in the middle of his garden, the Emperor looked out over Loyang. It was not really very impressive, but life had returned and he felt he had made good use of every minute. He began to ask questions of himself: 'What would have happened if I had been killed? Who would have accomplished all this?'

At that very moment, he felt someone push him from behind—and he fell straight into the stream. He turned round with a smile and saw the old Sage. 'You're thinking again, Emperor! It's not by thinking that you'll understand where you come from and where

you're going. Thinking is a means, like walking or eating your first meal. It's only a means—a first step or a first taste. You're right that it's a very important step and that you must learn to think—but you must also know how to stop thinking, since your convoluted cerebrations won't help your people or help you understand yourself!'

The Emperor smiled at the old Sage: 'Have I done what I was supposed to do?' he asked.

'What have you done?' replied the old Sage.

'Look at Loyang—the town has come back to life and I have given up all the stones in my palace to its reconstruction.'

'Was it not what you had to do?' asked the Sage.

'Was it what I was supposed to do?'

'Did you do it, yes or no?'

'Yes,' said the Emperor.

'Then it is what you had to do; it was a part of your true being. Why do you ask me that question?'

'Because I feel very lonely.'

'You feel lonely...Why?'

'I suppose I need someone to talk to,' said the Emperor.

'Talk to the people who are helping you!' said the Sage.

'But they're afraid of me,' said the Emperor.

'Why? Is it because you retreat to this garden or because you are Emperor?'

'I don't know,' said the Emperor.

'Let's go to Loyang,' said the Sage.

They left the garden and went into the streets of Loyang. The soldier who had helped the Emperor gave them a warm welcome, and so did the dyer; everybody smiled at the Emperor and the Sage and greeted them cordially. The Emperor noticed the child he had tried to carry away from the ruined buildings, and the little boy gave him a happy smile. As they walked through the streets of Loyang, he could feel the affection of the people all round and it made him very happy.

The Sage said to him: 'They're not afraid of you—they respect you. There's a subtle difference between fear and respect. These people respect you for what you are; before they were afraid of you, but now they respect you. *Use* that respect—don't hide yourself away in your garden, on your mountain or in a monastery or some out-of-the-way place where they can't see you. Respect is a sign that a being has evolved to its ultimate limit; it is due to the fact that an individual knows who he is.'

The Emperor turned to the Sage and said: 'I would like to have you with me all the time. You give me confidence and peace.'

The Sage smiled: 'The people around you feel exactly the same way about you.'

'What,' said the Emperor, 'they feel the same way about me as I do about you?'

'Yes,' said the Sage.

'I'd never thought of that!' the Emperor exclaimed.

'Why not?' asked the Sage.

'Because I'm only an Emperor and you're a Sage!'

'That's only a matter of terminology,' said the Sage. 'Whatever you are, use it!'

The Sage continued on his way, but the

Emperor remained in the middle of the street watching him disappear into the distance. He neither turned round nor looked back. He knew what he was, who he was, and that others needed to find the same confidence in themselves that he had helped the Emperor discover in himself; others needed to experience a similar illumination, to have someone they could regard not with fear but respect. Because respect allows evolution. It allows one to evolve towards knowledge without needing words; it allows one to become conscious of oneself.

A small boy came up to the Emperor as he watched the Sage moving away. He pulled at his sleeve and called out: 'Emperor!'

The Emperor turned towards him. 'What do you want?'

'Emperor, tell me—where do I come from?...'

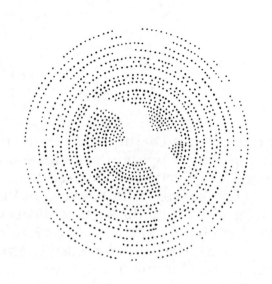

ISBN 0 85692 177 7

First published in 1984 under the title *Utilise Ce Que Tu Es* by Editions Soleil, Geneva, Switzerland

Translated by Mathew Reisz

Typeset by GCS, Leighton Buzzard, Beds.
Printed and bound in Great Britain by
WBC Limited, Bridgend, Mid Glamorgan.